Diary of A Madman

Diary of A Madman

Charlie Davis

Library of Congress Control Number   2009906363
ISBN: Hardcover   978-1-4415-4265-6
                     Softcover   978-1-4415-4264-9

To order additional copies of this book, contact:
Xlibris Corporation
1-888-795-4274
www.Xlibris.com
Orders@Xlibris.com
63978

What you about to read is eighty percent true and fifteen percent fiction. This was done to put some bite on a horrible account of the real. I hope you can understand how a young innocent man can be turn into a blood thirsty killer.

CHAPTER ONE

The story I'm about to tell is the truth as best I can tell. The names and places have been changed To protect the innocent and national security. Let's call me David Robinson and I was born November 1, 1952 in Mecklenburg County, Virginia. My parents were named Clarence and Mattie Robinson. My mother had a seventh grade education and my father had a sixth grade education. My parents expected all of us, my two sisters and me to do and go further in acquiring

an education and do better better in life than they

did. I attended the last of the old Field Schools, that

was disbanded in 1963. In 1967 I was one of the first

to attend the first integrated schools in Mecklenburg

County. I grew up in the South on the tailend of the Jim

Crow Era. In 1970, like blacks in the south did, I went

north, because there were nothing for blacks. I went

to Newark, New Jersey where I got a job working at a

hospital. Every two weeks when I got paid I faithfully

sent money home to my mother to help out. I met a

young Woman, with whom I thought I had feelings for.

It didn't work out. Vietnam War was going on and my

draft number was fast coming up.

CHAPTER TWO

As I previously stated, heart broken, my draft number fast coming up. I decided to join the United States Marine Corp. I reported July 30,1971 to PARRIS ISLAND, SOUTH CAROLINA. We took a bunch of Test verbal and written. All of a sudden I realized I didn't like being a Marine. I wanted to go out and I did everything possible to get out but it didn't work, I graduated from Boot Camp. I arrived at Camp Le Jeune, North Carolina for advance Basic Training. One day a captain came in barracks called five names, mine included march us into a bus, took us to another part of the base. We were in this room. Seventeen of us, the colonel got up in front of us and told us that we had been selected for the specialty service. Then they started calling names and said to follow them out of the room single file. When everybody was gone, I was the only one left. This Sgt. came over to me told me to go with him. We went outside, got into jeep and went to the Airstrip, got on a plane flew for about half hour. When we landed I was blind folded, put on a bus for 15 minutes arrived at a secret location. I was told to take off my blindfold. The next six months, I was trained counter terrorist tactics, hand to hand, trained as a sniper, as an assassin, how to make explosive devices, jump out of planes, hanging on a rope via copter. How to rapell down a cliff. We trained in the water, how to live off the land. Plus I already knew how to fly a helicopter, small plane, drive a tank, tractor trailer, Bus. We ran up to 15, 20, miles a day. Stood in the rain for hours holding first a rifle then a 50 pound. pack. They would take us out in the water with back pack about a mile from shore and leave us. We had to swim back. One guy didn't make it back. He came back in a body bag. We had jump out of the helicopter about 15 ft. in the air on land and about 25 feet over water. One guy broke his collar bone and another suffered a concession on a jump water.

CHAPTER THREE

The next step in our training was to be captured treated like prisoners of war. The military had this insane idea they could prepare us to cope with being prisoners of war. In my opinion, just personal thinking, it was failure of the worse kind, because you needlessly traumatized guys for no reason. The odds of you being capture was about two in fifteen. Most of the time, the enemy kills captives, cause it was less troublesome than to have to guard or feed live prisoners. The only prisoner they didn't kill were officers and soldiers they thought had valuable information that be useful to them.

We were put into bus with all the windows black taken to remote camp. Once there, they split us up in groups of three. I caught cage in the water up to your chin, which meant standing straight up so you wouldn't go under the water which became harder the longer you stood there. I stood there. I was there two days. Next, they moved me to the Tin house in the middle of the compound. Let me tell you its 95 degrees in that tin hut, it feels like 140 degrees, you think you was being roasted alive. I spend 24 hours in the hut. They put me in the wooden coffin then buried me alive. I was there 48 hours. I forgot to mention that each one of us before we got there was told a piece information. But the trick was one of the pieces was no good without all the pieces. Their job was to extract all the information from us. A it turns out, (I didn't know it) I was the last and most important piece of the puzzle. Next they hung me upside down for eight hours. I still didn't talk. According to the rules of the exercise there was nothing more they could do to me. I was the only one they didn't break. They were pissed, but there was nothing more they were allowed to do. After another 2 months, everybody was shipped to their first duty station. I was

shipped to a well known marine base south of the

Nation's capital. There I received instruction in counter

Insurgence and more training as an assassin.

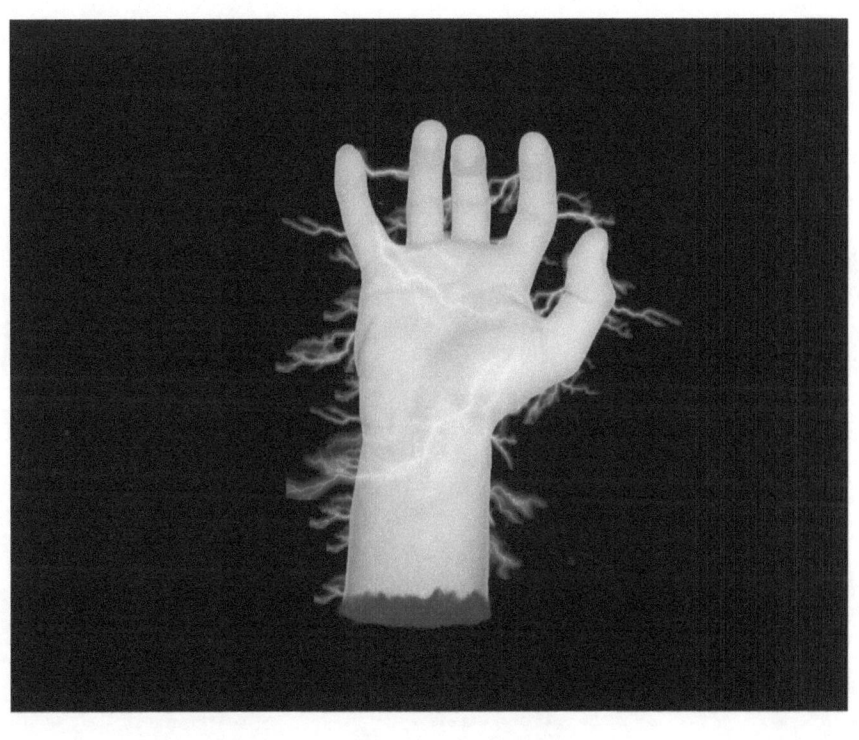

CHAPTER FOUR

My first assignment was to gather information and disable or take out terrorist cells operating in the Eastern United States. Of course we all know the government doesn't make deals with terrorist no matter how high the stakes were. There was the government employees who shall remain nameless, was being blackmail by certain terrorist group, to provide them with Top Secret document. The powers that be decided it was time to take care of this problem so they

agreed to pay the million dollars demand to release this

employee's mother. I was sent to deliver the money at

the drop site. I made the drop. Then left, but I didn't

go far. I had on a reversible jacket, which I reversed.

Put on a cap I had struck down the back of my pants,

then follow at a safe distant. What the man who made

the pick up didn't know that the briefcase was lined

with explosives to be remotely set off by me. We figured

the man would take the case back to his colleagues.

Indeed he did. Another thing they didn't know the

briefcase was bugged. I follow him back to their hide

out. After he went inside, I was able to listen to their

conversation. The one who made the pick up wanted to

open the case and count the money right away, but the

leader (I assumed was the leader) told him no hurry

that he trusted the USA government. Beside, if you

can't trust good US of A who could you trust? Instead

they started talking about the remain of their plan now

that they had the money which also including killing

their captive. Once I got the location, I call the boss

and report everything and got the OK to blow them up.

(I guess you thought I was nuts blowing up a million

dollar, HA HA it was counterfeited.) I detonated the

briefcase blowing the building up killing the inside.

Later going through their debris, we discovered that

the reason the whole joint blew up so completely was

cause they had explosive C-4+ Kerosene in the building.

How lucky can you get? That case wasn't as bad as

my next assignment. As a result of the info I collect

badly disable two cells operating in the Eastern part

of USA.

Chapter Five

My next assignment, I was sent to work undercover with the CID. I helped crack and bring down the Biggest military Black Market in the world. For two years I worked my way through the ring. Gathering Information of people, places and things. I started at the bottom on the island of Okinawa, Japan Operating out of Kadena Air Force Base(for those of who do not know this island very small only 60 miles long) doing business on the rock included drugs, loan sharking,

steal government supplies Such as Jeeps, Trucks, Cars

and guns. They would fly them on an Air Force Base

in Germany (which I won't name.) From there they

would be shipped to South America, the Middle East

and Africa. As I said I started in Okinawa and worked on

to Germany, the Middle East and United States. I found

out That this ring was very well organized from top to

bottom. It was struck like the mob, you had soldiers

Enforcers Lts. Captains, under boss. Then there the

inter circle. Made up of operation managers, chiefs,

And the Big Boss. Once I learn all parts, structures, of

the Ring, I had names, places, what, when and where.

We were ready Nov. 9th 1974 in early morning we struck

everywhere at once. We caught, Generals, Colonels,

Captains, Lts. And a host of enlisted people. We shut it

down form one end to the Other, dealing a serious blow

to the Black Market worldwide. After this assignment I

took a leave of a Absent for two months before being

reassigned.

CHAPTER SIX

There was this country next door to South Vietnam in which a certain Warlord has been for years Running wild. The United States needed to have somebody more favorable to the U.S. in power. They needed this for years the enemy crossed back and forth across the border between Vietnam and Well known country (which I shall not name.) So, they decide to assassinate the leader of these people And install a leader favorable to the U.S. and would stop the enemy

troops from this country as a hideout or base. Myself

and three other men was selected to carry out this

task. The terrain was bad and tribement and troops

was very ruthless. You would be shot on sight, hanged

and skinned, or beheaded, boiled in oil. We set out

into the countryside, very carefully and slowly making

our way to the rebels camp. Using military intelligence.

We traveled for the better part of three days, before

reaching camp. We lost one man on the way (Booby

trap). We sat up and waited for an opportunity to carry

out our plan. Finally our chance came. I got him lined

up in my gun's sight, fired one round, striking him

in the back of the head. All hell broke loose. Bullets

were flying everywhere. We were out-numbered four to

one. We lost another man (shot). The other man and

me rapidly retreated at a high rate of speed. My buddy

stepped wrong broke his ankle and fractured his foot.

I had to carry him on my back for 50 miles being chase

by the enemy all the way. We safely made if back over

the border into Vietnam. I didn't realized I hurt my

back. The doctor said because of the adrenalin rush

I didn't feel it Until I calm down and reached safety. I

spent the next week in traction. For two months I had

to walk Like a duck, twice day in the whirlpool. Before

I finally got better. If you think this mission was a trip,

Wait until I tell you about the next one.

CHAPTER SEVEN

After I got better in my back. I was sent to a certain Marine base south of Washington D.C. as an in Instructor on hand to hand combat. For six months, then taught in the classroom the theory of terrorist Tactics 101. After four months, I was assigned to a certain big name government agency in Washington D.C. Starting with the third letter of the alphabet. I took care of their loose ends, made certain things go away. Their dirty work so to speak. I was sent to a certain country in South America to tie up some loose ends. Acting on the info given me I attempt to carryout the my mission. Unknown to me that I had bad intell walked into a trap, was captured. I was taken deep in the jungle to a captives camp. They put me in a pit with 300 poisonous snakes, all kinds, big ones, little ones, and medium size ones. Thank god that at the time I was heavily into meditation. I put myself into a trace for two days. I sat motionless for two days not moving a muscle. If I had moved I would have been bitten hundreds of times. That why to this day I fear snakes. I have nightmares about snakes. Then they took me out of the snake pit (they used fire extinguishers on the snakes) to get me safely out. They put me in a wooden box, buried me alive for 72 hrs. then removed me from the box, hung me upside down took a water hose constantly running the The water on me. You had to keep your eyes close, water went in your nose, ears + mouth. This Continue for hours, I lost count how many. Then there was this big explosion all around the camp, then Helicopter, gunships came into the camp blasting away with their cannon. Then I was being cut down, Help to a waiting helicopter and we left. As a result of being buried in a box underground today I have Fear of tight dark spaces.

There was another case, where I helped foil a plot to set off dirty explosion devise in the subway systems in NEW YORK CITY and PHILADELPHIA, PA. I went

under cover to gather information on two local based

(home grown terrorist). My contact put me in touch

with MR. JONES, who hooked me up with a man that

went by the name of MING, who took me to his boss,

who shall remain nameless. They were looking for

someone to make a dirty explosive device for them.

After they dropped me off, I cleverly planted tracking

on the van. Myself and another agent followed them

around for almost a week before I was contacted. hey

came picked me up at the agreed upon site they took

to their secret place. Dirty explosive devices are not

hard to make if you know your chemistry. You can buy

everything you need over the counter. I put together

what they thought was explosive dirty devices (but, they

was not, did you really think I WAS GOING to make

the real thing.). Instead I made a harmless device that

smelled bad make your nose run and your eyes water,

I put a tracking device in them. We waited until they

set their plan in motions, then we follow them, cause

if you remembered I had planted tracking device on

their van, and we had followed them all over the place

gathering information, taking pictures. While I was

there at their hideout I planted a listening device. We

heard all their plans, so we knew exactly all their plans.

Then we made our move, swept them all up in a nice

neat package.

CHAPTER EIGHT

I served in the Marine Corps two yrs. Active duty. Then they took me off the book. At this point there is A couple ways they can do this. They can list you as missing in action, accidental death body not re-Covered or close coffin burial, or inactive reserve. Sometimes active reserves. They arrange covers for You, set you up in government jobs, sometimes civilian jobs, change your name. After I went off book They put me in the inactive reserves for four years, I went home to a government job, went on assignments as needed. Then I went for years active reserves, and continued the same way, taking missions as needed. Last five years after getting out of the Marines for good. I worked special operations under this well known government agency in Washington D.C. tying up loose ends, taking care of special problems, gathering info anywhere or any way I could get it.

CHAPTER NINE

I went to this certain midwest city on information that there was going to be an attempt on the President of U.S.A. wife. We surround the hideout of the middle east terrorist cell. We captured everyone inside. The interrogation tactics not exactly legal, we found out that the explosive device was under the stage (this was outside). The device was found, time was running out, we decide to get the device out some place where it could blowup harmlessly. I volunteered to drive it to a picked location. The local law enforcement ran interference. I got to this big vacant lot with seconds to spare. After this assignment I started to become more unstable. I was have trouble sleeping, the night-mares were get worse. I could hear voices sometimes, see things that were not there. The agency knew all this, and did nothing, Kept sending me on assignments. Soon I started to drink and experimenting with drugs. But functional that's all they was concern about. Over the next two years, I kept getting worse. The agency knew all of this, still did nothing to help me. So I started to seeing a head doctor (Whom I thought was reporting everything I said, my condition in general). After six months, they put me on the Retired list and cut me off. Burnt me as they say in the business. After I got out I continue to see a Head doctor for almost a year before I gotten a good job working for a government contractor. I worked There for eight years. Then really started getting unstable again in a big way. I lost my job, my house, car and all the money in the bank. My family was dumbfounded. By 1991 I was completely homeless, cut-off from family and friends, I isolated, drank and drugged. I slept in doorways, parks, bus stops, trash dumpsters. I lived in a big card board box, bandtaminiums (abandon buildings). This continue for the next ten years on and off. Finally 2001, I went into the VA ran program for homeless Veterans I stayed about a year and left, two months later I was back using

on the street again. This time my family thought I was

crazy and gave up on me. It wasn't until 2003, I moved

to Baltimore Maryland I got in a privately run program

for homeless Vets. It was the best move I made in the

last ten years or so. It wasn't until I was fully diagnosed

with paranoid schizophrenia, rage issues, and manic

depression I stayed at the VA for eight months, I got

better with medication and staying clean. Today I'm

doing fine I have a loving wife and step son who loves

me a lot. When I was homeless and on drugs I had

this prayer I used to recite each night before I went to

sleep with a metal bar in my hand to ward off rats twp

legged and four legged if you know what I mean. Oh!

Boy its this fool your humble servant talking to you one more time. Man am I tired and sick. People just don't understand how it is out here. My body drugged out on crack and crank and my soul tired. Give me the strength to survive out here in this crazy world. I'll be talking to you tomorrow night if you're listening.

CHAPTER TEN

People just don't understand how it is to be homeless. They think you are lazy, don't want to do any Better, you're subhuman an animal of some kind. People are homeless for a number of reasons some Are, they lost their job, they have mental health issues, alcoholics, drugs (legal or illegal). It's not just Single people anymore, its whole family, women and children, little children. While I was homeless People spit on you, throw money at you, act like you was invisible, the cops

hassle you most places Of business won't even let in the

door and if they do someone follows you around until

you leave. Certain hoods in town you can't go, cause

they call the cops, to chase you out. Seventy-five percent

of all homeless people are disable veterans (physical

+ mental). This country treats its veterans worse than

any other country in the world. I wrote this book

because I felt I had a story to tell (its long over due).

I decided why should I tell me story to a head doctor

for nothing. When if I write about it, may—get paid for

it. Cause I feel I paid my dues. For fifteen years I gave

up everything for country and flag. I was one sad sob.

I killed so many I loss count after 22. My family if they

knew the truth they would be proud of me. I had a hell

of a ride for a old country boy from Virginia. Ever wake

at night can't go back to sleep? Hearing three voices

talking to all at once very loudly, the walls seems to be

moving, closing in around you. Other nights you hear

a whole chorus of voices, screaming, laughing, crying

and shouting. Experiencing quick flashes of pictures,

of walking thru fields of rothed bodies, all decated.

Running in the woods being chased by something

you don't see. Hearing voices telling you to do this

and that. As a result of this I have to take three kinds

of sleeping pills to knock me out all night long. Then

I wake up in the morning angry and don't know why,

or very depressed, don't like crowds of people. I like

being by myself. I don't go to funerals, cause I can't stand to look at the dead bodies. I have nightmares if I do. I don't like guns, knives and I don't like violence. I like peace and quiet I don't sleep in a dark room with the door closed. I keep the door open when I go to the bathroom. I I take 15 pills a day. I'm getting better as time progress. Slowly but surely I am. Over the years I felt my Life between 18 and 48 was wasted. I felt I hadn't got much achieved . Only until maybe a couple of years ago, did my feelings changed. My sisters and me are finally talking to one another. I finally am getting to know some of my children. Oh by the way all turned out all right I got 4 teachers, I doctor, 1 cop, 1 realtor, 1 beautician, 1 career military man not bad.

I hope after you read this book you'll have a better understanding of the mighty workings of this country.I didn't intend to bring harm to anyone, call anybody out, so to speak. It was just something I spent a lot of years thinking about and finally got up enough nerve to write it. Since you read my story, make what you want of it, draw your own conclusions. Cause I told the truth so help me God. Anything I got I earned. Nobody owes me nothing. I earned it all paid in full. My family and children will be proud of me and my accomplishments. While I was in service, in my spare time long before computers and online, there was home study, where colleges would mail you your assignment, you would complete them, send them back, and wait for your next lesson to be sent. As a result of that, I amasted enough credits to get two associate degrees. Two separate colleges, one in chemistry, the other is in communications. I also got my GED too. In the fall, I plan to go back to college and get my Masters Degree.

This book is dedicated to the memory of my parents, Clarence and Mattie Bell Davis and also to my sisters Correne and Berta, whom I love very much.